Correspondence

Kathleen Graber

Winner of the 2005 Saturnalia Books Poetry Prize
Selected by Bob Hicok

saturnalia books

Correspondence

Kathleen Graber

saturnalia books

Saturnalia Books
105 Woodside Rd.
Ardmore, PA 19003
info@saturnaliabooks.com

ISBN 0-9754990-3-3

Book Design by Saturnalia Books
Printing by The Prolific Group, Canada.

Cover Art: "Horse Against Studio Wall, 1999" by Rosamond W. Purcell © 2004 R.W. Purcell

Author Photograph: Francis Kaklauskas

Distributed by:
Small Press Distribution
1341 Seventh Street
Berkeley, CA 94710-1409
1-800-869-7553

Acknowledgments from Kathleen Graber:

I would like to acknowledge the following journals in which several poems first appeared: *Ploughshares*,
Green Mountains Review, *The Hudson Review*, *Washington Square*, *Bucks County Review*, *Tiferet*, *Arts &
Letters*, and *Dragonfire*.

I am grateful to the New Jersey State Council on the Arts and the Rona Jaffe Foundation for their gener-
ous support.

I have many people to thank, beginning with Bob Hicok, and Henry Israeli and Joanna Goodman at
Saturnalia Books, and Rosamond Purcell, who so generously provided the photograph that appears on the
cover. I owe an enormous debt to the writing communities at New York University. The poets who were
my classmates in the Creative Writing Program—Kazim Ali, Adam Day, K. Dimma, Brian McDonald, Jason
Schniederman, and Adam Williams—have been unwavering in their support and exceptionally generous
with their feedback. I want to thank our director and tireless advocate, Melissa Hammerle, for her deep
kindness and encouragement. My teachers, at NYU and elsewhere, have been amazing poets and exempla-
ry human beings: Renee Ashley, Stephen Dunn, Galway Kinnell, Peter Murphy, and Tom Sleigh. I feel pro-
foundly fortunate to teach in NYU's Expository Writing Program, and I want to thank Pat Hoy, a writer
and thinker from whom I have learned so much. I want especially to thank Mark Doty for not only his
consistently intelligent insights but also for his abiding optimism and unshakable belief in me. My deep
thanks also to Paul Lisicky for his warm and truly delightful friendship. My thanks to Aaron Balkan, Ciaran
Berry and Anthony Carelli, Barbara Daniels, and Elinor Mattern for the careful attention that they have
brought to every poem I've ever shown them. Every writer imagines an ideal reader. My deepest thanks to
Matt Donovan for having been all that that implies, incredibly patient, smart, honest, and inspiring.

Finally, to my family—Joan and Len, Francis and, Elizabeth, Erin and Colleen—and my dear friend Frank
Smigiel—for their ongoing support. And beneath even this, to my husband Larry, whose steadiness and
love have made this book possible.

For the dead—

Bud and Eileen Kalafski
Edward Kalafski
Len and Angelina Klaus
Margaret Henderson

Contents

One

Two

Three

Perhaps the most deeply hidden motive of the person who collects can be described this way: he takes up the struggle against dispersion. Right from the start, the great collector is struck by the confusion, by the scatter, in which the things of the world are found.

Every passion borders on the chaotic, but the collector's passion borders on the chaos of memories.

—Walter Benjamin

One

The houses turn from the tracks & play instead,
nose to nose with their identical neighbors,
                                    the same old games:
who will blink first, guess what I'm hiding behind my back. How long
have they held the mower, the buried bone, the hubcap
in their yards? Someone's saving seven busted up rowboats
a long way from the sea. Isn't this art, this careful arrangement of what is
useless?
            The way *Painting Without Mercy* emerges
on broken plates. Even if there were water, a flood, nothing here
would float. Even from the train, we can tell a story
about the epiphanic suffering
                                of saints, even from here we can see the split
wood, the violent gray gash in the bow, give them names—*Lucy,*
Patron of Hide and Seek, Sophia, Martyr
of the Twenty Questions.
                            And this is where we stop, waiting
for the signal from the station. It's a tired trope, a bright February.
I've lost something
                        I'll never find. This is about black & white television,
about Ed Sullivan in earnest conversation with Topo Gigio,
acting as though he didn't know there was a script,
a human hand inside. I don't want to suggest
the assemblagist's religion of junk because maybe
                                                it's simpler,
the explanation for what's collecting
                                    beyond the fence—
an ancient urge that rises up from the base of the skull & ferries us
to the harvest of whatever we can. But I spy a red rowboat on sawhorses
in the morning of every day. Somebody come tell me
that's not a kind of faith.
                            Somebody say that's not the kind of sign
we should expect from a god.

Terra Incognita

My dog does everything three times now,
                              the circling, the sniff.
She takes the food into her mouth & drops it, takes it,
drops it again, until it is all out of the bowl, the little kibbles
spread around the table legs or spun off
beneath the stove.
                    And then, suddenly recalling her hunger,
she hunts down the ones she can.
                                My father wanted to talk about his death,
but I wouldn't let him. I blame the Phillies' poor pitching.
If the Eagles had had a better draft that year, the outcome
might have been much different.
                            I want to deny the way our interest in things
can run away.
            During a kickoff, he told me
that it is possible to fall in & out of love many times, sometimes
with the same person, sometimes not. He said
he could feel himself coming apart,
                                & when my brother began to sob,
I told him:
            Dad, look what you've done.
You have to stop.
                The dog is old; she's lost her sense of smell.
It's that very, very slow
                        fading away, like walking out
into the morning sun, blinking a little, having forgotten
exactly how, exactly why.
                        The aromas of chicken soup & liver
no longer call her to the kitchen.
                            Yellow cheese on yellow tile eludes her;
she snorts & slavers, snuffles an inch or two

to the right. Yet on the walk, in the park, she does
what dogs always do:
                      she buries her breathing head in the leaves
& straw, brushes her nostrils against the trunks of trees & hydrants.
I've seen her lick the grass & bark, taste the ground, lead
snake-like with her tongue.
                            My father wouldn't try. What slipped away
he wanted to release. Twice, he asked why my mother wasn't there.
He seemed asleep
                  even when he wasn't. He said the world is hiding,
& it is.

Romantic Museum

For days I have felt that familiar gravity. Spring again?
The worlds aligned? Andromeda, like an insomniac in brightness,

glued awake to the false opening
at the back of the box.
                              It will pass. I'm waiting

for a buzzer to sound—
the words of the day: *speech act.* What if everything you say

is said with cunning & beauty, & everything I say is
the same? What we say will never be said.
                                        Having been said meaning

arrived—not on the stoop
like a package in the rain, but in,
                              dry, flat letter through the slot.

At dawn, the flakes come down,
the way snow suspends & drops on souvenir New York Cities

or catches along the thin struts of a tiny Eiffel Tower
in its shaken dime-store dome. *City of Light.*
                              East of the Turnpike,

just yesterday, empty storage containers the size of railcars
advertised themselves for rent. Stacked like a child's colored blocks,

they climb six high, four deep, above the industrial meadow
so that the abandoned brick depots around them look—

all the windows black & pane-less—
like Cornell's grand hotels, shrunken outs: *Etoile, Cygne,*

Setting for a Fairy Tale. Once upon a dark, dark time....
What is it about ruin
                    that lures us? What is it in you I sidle beside?

I have a friend who has fallen in love
for the first time in a long time, & in a dream her lover

is *transmogrified*—becomes a fawn.
                         Hmmm..., we say, *vulnerability.*
Hmmm... tenderness.
                    All my life I have practiced

reading between the lines, & I can find there anything
imaginable, impossible, & nothing, too—

or not nothing,
                    what feels like it though, the terror
of never finding myself again

collecting in a different mouth.
                             My friend confides that her new lover
is her muse. Perhaps, she adds, I have forgotten how

a *newness* feels.
                    Joseph Cornell lined his basement with the exhausted:
cartons of almost-worthless windfall

never meant to last. We can scarcely make ourselves consider
what it was he craved, what wingless nightmare he exorcised

inside each frame.
                    There is *attention* within me,
still unscattered, unspent, & with it, I fall

in & out all the time.
                    We wouldn't call it *love*.
I have been married such a long time. What

can I know about the rest? Downpours seen through glass.
You? The storm's fresh eye or, more truly, only the idea of eye,

the idea of ear, of tongue. Sprung—
I fly out, safe, into the wet, evacuated street.
                              I have made a muse

of the near-nothing of not knowing
if I like it this way: to never tell

what it is I mean.
              Accumulation, the fierce third rail buried
alive beneath the tracks.
                    From the road, who can imagine

each box big enough to live in? Any one could hold
everything I've got.
                  Later, an afternoon sun breaks out & I wander uptown,

buying asparagus & a large orange, & they bounce in their small bag
like a broken doll,
                  or only its bright, heavy head

& a green grove of pick-up sticks. Tomorrow the round cup in my hand
will be the warm belly of a bird; the yolk shimmying in the pan,

a summer moon
                rising up into a peppered white photo-negative of stars.
Sometimes I dream a great bear. Sometimes ice,

a corrugated warehouse,
every hinge sealed shut.
                But last night I dreamt you simply

as yourself. For aren't we even stranger as we really are?
                                        Jewel casket.
Apothecary jar. Perhaps sand. Perhaps something

other.
        Each grain unopenable & accruing. In a universe more space
than material, even the atom held together merely by attraction,
                                                I am

the same *trespass*: barely bound,
                dishonest, sincere, yours, unread.

The Work of Art in the Age of Mechanical Reproduction

Trust me:
my happiness bears
no relation to happiness.

—Taha Muhammad Ali

At thirty, a woman wants to have a child, but

she will never have one.

Doctors will pump her empty belly with air, make

the small incisions, put a camera in. More than once,

she will drive a hundred miles with her husband's sperm
in a glass vial warmed between her thighs

& inject herself with hormones

distilled from the urine of mares. Month in, month out,

the twin engines of the ovaries work a follicular double-time.

The woman

behind the counter at Unique Copy Center calls me *baby*.

I'm not the kind of woman who'd call anybody *baby*,

not even the baby I never had. *Baby,* she asks, *is this clear enough*
for you? You know, we can make these real

high resolution, if that's what you want.

She's wearing a shiny pendant with the face of a little girl
printed directly onto the disc.
                              It looks

like an archaic daguerreotype—although Daguerre's prints,

on their polished silver surfaces, were so much harder to see.
What does Benjamin tell us
                              about *the aura of the authentic*? It bears,

he says, in its singularity the terrible wear of its past. If I ever wanted

a child, I wanted what I was taught to want. This is how we re-read
our lives. I read that I never wanted a child. You may read

I am only telling myself I didn't want what I could not have.

But we have words: we recognize
                              correspondence,
conception, rationale, repair. One poet says *we need names.*

Every child must know all the birds in the yard. For what would we do

if we did not know the names of the ten thousand things?
                                             Another says,
When I go into the wood and see a flower I do not know, I consume it.

I bring it into the womb of the mind, where it can grow.

And when it has grown, I bless it. I give it the name
I think it should have. Cabinet des Mirages. Passage du Desir. Luna.

Looking Glass. For Benjamin, the names are never merely signs. A woman

in her thirties wanted a child; the woman in her forties
can barely recall her.
                    Perhaps it's not words that fail, but memory—

the amber ampoule, the brittle bulb from which we struggle

to extract the drug. Not memory that fails, but
the needle of our grammar.
                         I have no rhetoric for this woman

I carry inside me. She had no syntax for the woman inside her.

Daguerreotype, Szarkowski says,
                         we must approach *in private, by lamplight,*
because it is
              elusive—a secret, its case half-closed. Take it in. Trust me:

the woman I am bears no relation to the woman I am.

After a Student, 15, Declares He Will Renounce the World for God

Down past the rusting Dodge, the forsythia shakes its blooms, says,
Look,
     I'm forever. I'm all the evidence you need.
I'm trying to remember when it was this easy to just give up
the world. Because now
                  I want it all. Every broken brick:
if not the fruit, the flower, if not this, the rind, whatever it is
that's left over.
           Bruegel's Babel—how the gods must stop here
at their own reflections. Scaffold, winch, lever, ladder.
Builders. I want to be the little one, with the bowl of mortar,
the third tier up—
           or is it the fourth?—riding the arch. Voussoirs,
intrados, the rise, the span—a kind of miracle,
                    that thin roof
over nothing. Tomorrow
           the yellow blaze gives way to leaves.
Of course, it does. But so do we. At the black door,
we open our mouths. We speak in tongues. From lip to lip,
there is only this
        beautiful confusion.

The Letters: A Mnemonic for Forgetting

L is for Laburnum

> *During his final illness (tuberculosis of the larynx)*
> *at the sanatorium in Kierling, Kafka was not supposed to speak....*
> *He communicated... by scribbling notes on slips of paper.*
> —Max Brod

1

The neighbors' son, clean & pajama-ed, stands at the screen door,
his wet hair still retaining his mother's careful part. In one hand,

he holds his bedtime bottle, in the other an old-fashioned toddler's toy:
a strand of jumbo, plastic, snap-together beads.

So much between us

remains unfinished. In a dream
you are speaking. We move a little
closer, still
I cannot hear what you say. When asked whether Felice

had ever really known him, Kafka scrawls, *as far as it was worth*
understanding me....She was not beautiful,
but slender.

It's an almost perfect spring 5:30— cool & light, despite the rain. Grass
has forced itself up again
between sidewalk cracks, & near the curb,

a stalk of dandelion & a small purple-flowering
                                    weed. To describe
his consumption on a conversation slip, he draws a picture with notes:

in the middle a faceted stone, at the side
                        the saws, otherwise everything
empty....
        We can live for years suspecting sleep might be a cure—

                            2

though the undeniable re-surfaces:
                        what we throw into the river, lashed up
in its burlap sack, keeps clawing its way toward our noontimes.

Soon it bobs along: its corpus as resilient on the ripples of day as a bright,
inflated lung.
            I know a man who has loved for decades a woman

who has ceased to care.
                        She's moved to another state, married
a different man, delivered dark-haired daughters & dark-haired sons.

Yet in unoccupied minutes, he can't stop himself from remembering
the way their bodies twisted together
                        or one of her small off-hand remarks.

He imagines her now,
                each day a sip of such spectacularly simple joy
that her happiness becomes for him, again & again, the same

unshutable wound.

        Yesterday evening a late bee drank the white lilac
dry. In the end, Kafka couldn't swallow enough food or water to stay alive,

but there were the flowers:
           the peonies, *because they are so fragile....*
Then please lightly spray the peonies... please see the peonies don't touch

3

the bottom of the vase. Show me the columbine, he insisted, *too bright*
to stand with the others.
        Scarlet hawthorn is too hidden, too much in the dark.

Can't laburnum be found? Later tonight
           I will run over two cats making love
on a black side street, recognize the inexact percussion of bone

beneath wheel. I will never see them nor hear their cries,
           lost
at that moment, no doubt, ... lulled into recalling... what?
           Any other time.

For Kafka, the Sirens are silent: their silence *a more fatal weapon*
than their song. But still
        Ulysses defies them, his ears stopped against

even that which remains unsung.
        We lean our heads so close I feel your lips
& the wind of your words against the mouth of my ear,
        but there is no sound.

You must be saying the obvious—everything I already know
                                        I don't want
to understand. At the doorstep of the waking world,
                                        regarding you,

I chose to be cut aslant, to go on dreaming. *It was a bargain*
made in half-sleep.... I promised
                        but now I have forgotten what.

Two

After Columbus Day, the shore towns close up so quickly
        no one bothers to pull in the signs. Postcards yellow
    all winter in windows beside a shell box, beside

t-shirts, plastic shovels, & pails. In my mother's house,
        I prepare to make things
                        disappear. I ask
    into the phone, *Who knew it would take so long*

to settle an estate? All around, the things she's saved have their say.
        But what do they say? Each day, they talk more & more
    only about themselves: red-lettered Chinese fortunes

in a drawer, as evocative as the dividend stubs around them.
        Fidelity Trust. An old dog will learn new tricks.
    My mother's x-rays. Months past their usefulness,

I still drive around with these images in my trunk:
        radiographs of the dead. *Memento mori*—
    who doesn't like the way it sounds? Or *uranium*?

Atomic number 92, that made these pictures possible,
                        all *celluloid*
        & *heft*. The off season: too early,
    too late, for anything you want to do. Afternoon's end,

that last curb before the street gives way to sand.
                        What can we say
        about our private sadness? The spine,
    its small white fists, three ribs around a fog of lung,

& her brain from every angle—although all the thoughts
              have gone. *You will visit a distant land*. Night:
       a rented film, or home movies on vacation

from the closet shelf in their little yellow Kodak cans. 1964.
              And my mother is *dressed*, as though life were
       an occasion, as though *fashion were the soul made visible*—

a claim that holds us because we want to prove all the ways
              it's flawed. I press rewind,
       & Annette Benning collapses again into hanger clatter—

not the last scene, but the almost over.
                            My niece
              safeguards my dead brother's ties in a plastic pouch
       that travels with her. But when she opens it, is anything…

regained? The vanished other? The lost, un-see-able self? Alchemy,
              maybe, half memory, half
                            silk.
              Marianne Moore's living room, her sofa, her phonograph,

the books on her shelf, in the order she put them,
              in their permanent place at the Rosenbach
       in Philadelphia. And there is a photograph there, too,

of the same room, before it was
                            moved. We have to keep
              checking ourselves. We're so tempted to play—
       the photo, the room, the photo… to keep on discovering

what's not there. My mother's heart was so strong I could see it
              beneath the blankets bang against the wall
       of her chest. I must have thought *a thing like that*

will just go on forever. Wind—the house rocks
                on its shallow footings—& home. What frightens me
        frightens me here
                        only a little less. The sky seems more.

The night-heron, duplicitous fisher, bends her long legs
                to the tide. The stars are brighter, but the dark fills up.
        The wise believe in magic. In a flicker, *poof*, my mother

pops up from below the water of a pool—& waves.
                We make the impossible possible; then
        it changes back. Somehow when we have to bury each other,

we do. She has become an Esther Williams bathing cap:
                wide white chin strap neatly snapped—
        around her head,
                        a rubbery halo of elaborate pink blooms.

Equivalent Difference

...*the best dictionary of Eskimo gives just two roots:*
qanik for snow in the air and aput for snow on the ground.
—George A. Miller, *The Science of Words*

Snow so exact it's clockwork, ticking precisely one inch
each hour, or snow without tempo, the frantic stomp,
then a crawl. A woman walks with the Lord through a blizzard
toward the PATH station. He wants to go up University,
across 9th, but she tells Him she knows a better way.
It can't be any shorter, He argues. The city's essentially a grid.
Lately, she confides, she's grown tired of the literal.
She's stopped dyeing her hair, & now, each day,
she surveys herself becoming what she's secretly become—
that white emerging. She never believed all of those stories

about the Eskimo words for snow, but she knows
the liturgy of erasure—the perfected stumblings
of the cells are called forward from the dark & named.
Turning west, she invents a new taxonomy: snow, at first,
as fine as netting and, then, the snow of the ball gown,
voluminous & billowing. He knows, of course,
that the street she has chosen won't get them there sooner,
but He enjoys bickering—especially over the inevitable
couple of yards. Another gust blows from the north.
The sidewalks disappear. Snow that slips in overnight

like a premonition, that accumulates slowly... like laundry,
like a drift of odd socks. She wonders if omniscience
might not be its own limitation. *Sub specie aeternitatis*—
but what kind of wisdom hasn't clutched its own heart
at the brink of the abyss? He says He understands

how this route past the park might seem to her quicker,
but if she'd planned ahead, they could have really saved time
by just cutting through. Sometimes how things seem
seems to be what's important. If she could preserve herself
wholly, she assures Him, she would. Winded, she stoops

to tighten her wet laces. In the silent window of the drugstore,
they study their reflections. A snow that would cover—an alibi,
the bleached bedding. And after a thaw, only a few slushy patches
tossed around like rough cotton rags. Or slender & refrozen
in the moonlight: stiff on the lawn as a mummy's soiled ribbon.
She points to the glass, reminded, she tells Him, again,
that the body we see is the body we own. He tells her,
one translator of the Bible converted the image of Christ
into the image of a seal. There's a linguistic theory:
equivalent difference, but still no word in Eskimo for lamb.

The Language of Bees

Across the street, a woman with two sleeves of tattoos

stands at the edge of the porch & shakes out a light blue rug. A small boy
in swim trunks races back & forth behind her.
                                        We go wrong mostly

by insisting the world is rimmed with un-erasable truths. Or

we go wrong by insisting the opposite:
                                        that surely it's not.
When Kierkegaard renounced his engagement to Regine,

he cast himself as the seducer. This lie, he thought, would be easier;

it was the truth
                he thought she would need. If only she'd known
the calculation of his actions, she would have recognized

his love. A swarm of bees has nested in the attic,

& even though I'm frightened & I want them gone,
I force myself to put my ear to the wall & listen: buzz-drill

of the *Rundtanz* & the *Schwanzeltanz*, the circling & wagging waltzes

described by Karl von Frisch. Dictionary of distance & direction—
the only part of speech, the body
                                turning. Half the time I want

what no one wants, what's scavenged: a quilt of tight, soft cotton.

This bit of housedress, a patch of someone's summer
                                                pajamas.
Walking at dawn, it's almost too easy to find something to love

in a neighbor's trash. Imagine a code.
                              A jumble of chipped clay pots:

I once held such tender pleasures. Chenille spreads
tied up with a plugless cord. Two chrome bar stools:
                                        Meet me later.

A sentence of things. The facts of this life as best I know them:

a colander, a shoebox of hinges, a cupboard door. Kierkegaard,
Lukacs tells us, *made from life a form*.
                              He wanted to live by *gesture,*

to make unambiguous & permanent a paradox of the heart.

And when, finally, he hoped to explain, she returned his letter
unread.
          Some days, I'm reckless, & some days, I board each thought

as though it were a cross-town bus, the destination guaranteed

by the familiar initials along its brow.
                                  Outside, the woman re-centers
a yellow sprinkler & rubber hose on her narrow, dusty lawn,

& the boy, on her signal, twists with both hands the spigot

that sends an arc of water
                          stuttering into the air. Bees navigate
by sunlight, by pollen, by the unmistakable nectar-scent.

Here is the way from the comb to the sweetness: three hundred meters

east to the cyclamen, twenty yards north to the phlox.

Oracle, With Lines from Montale's
"La Farandola Dei Fanciulli"

"You in love with love,
but you don't act on it—
because you are afraid.
And you should be.
You too old—
When you seventeen,
you can get your heart broke
by the nightshift busboy,
but you don't fall
for some young thing now—
when you thirty-five."

Because the diner is always open, you will go there—
by the railroad, up back of the beach
                             to listen to the waitresses
talking among themselves (perhaps you are too happy, too unhappy, perhaps
you cannot sleep), to put a book down,
                                 open on the counter, as though you are reading,
but because it is hard to read in times like these,
weeds suddenly breaking into blossom,
                           to look only at the words
spread out on the page, *a flowering of thirst.*

"Just because he dance you
'round the kitchen when it slow
to some swing, jitterbug bullshit song
that come on at 2 am, & you,
you don't never know
how to dance before—
your one hand in his & the other
waving in the air

like you on some parade float—
you forget yourself.
You think you something new."

It's as if being naked and nameless
was being sunlight, flower, heat-shimmer.
You won't look up for fear they will stop
                              saying what they are saying,
& most times, what they say will be
what you will have to hear.
                    How far back the ancient past seems now.

"I know you thinking
you can teach this boy some things,
but there ain't no secret kinda kiss
to make him crazy about you.
And if there was, God know,
you wouldn't be the woman
to be knowing it."

Sometimes you will think there is so little pleasure
we must snatch it,
On the gravel and cinders of the railbed, sometimes
                              so little sway—

The Letters: A Mnemonic for Forgetting

E is for Elegies, or Enough to be Counted

> *...the poet deliberately, skillfully, insouciantly, cunningly, faithfully, unforgivably forgets. It is the only kind of forgetting which is also a form of remembering....*
> —Larry Levis

1

Another pink evening. The tired calliope of the first ice cream truck
churns away down a different block. And then,
                              what I think must be

the breath of a machine I cannot recognize
                              becomes a slender, imperfect v
of geese honking north. Because, just an hour before, there'd been a cardinal

in a tree & a squall of starlings, the whole earth for a moment seems *wing*
& *flutter*
            so that even the stones driven up against a cement stanchion at sunset

appear to me impossibly round & fragile, expectant skin,
as patient in their dirty nest of sand & wrappers as a pigeon's mislaid eggs.

I'm not in love with anyone anymore, Levis writes in '83.
But the form of stone is the form of attrition:
                              it becomes itself

through what is lost, the way tumbling a song on a jukebox
quarter after quarter will make you blind to its music—
                                        annihilation,

we might call it, by a brutal, adolescent
                              affection, that other circuit
to forgetting, as implausible as it might seem, the width of memory

like a record's groove un-inscribing itself with use. *We*
in the most threadbare hotel room in Missouri, when the light was out,

                              2

were touch,…and our bodies had the textures of wind….
                                        Last night
I forgot my keys on the back seat of the cab. I stood in the hall a long time

searching my pockets, the bottom of my bag. Yet when I rushed out,
the driver was still there, logging the night's accounts into his ledger.

Dumb luck: a thing to remember to be thankful for—how the small coincidence
can sometimes make the late hours sweet—
                              how it allows us to allow

that there's still a little time
                    to consider our mistakes, a minute for returning
& undoing
          whatever it is we're so afraid we've done. Even in May,

the dead are all around us.
                              Slipping between an overgrown hedge & an oak,
walking home from the bay, I was stopped last week by the delicate,

rigid body of a bird: its back precisely snuggled into the root-lift, its legs,
thin as bass strings, pushed stiffly away from its mottled breast—

what must have been
                              a flecked & lovely flashing, almost weightless
in the leaf-shadow. A marsh wren, maybe, that streak of white

3

across the crown.
                       I caught myself bending down to lift it, tempted, just then,
to bring it home—without even pausing to wonder why or how, or why, again.

And still, I half-want to go back and find it,
                                          alive now, as I know it must be,
in its belly with other lives:
                              the dangerous, disturbing mechanics of decay.

*Maybe to be 'in love' is to love something that passes, which speaks solemnly
to you just once,*
                which is like wind with its texture.... I'd rather forget

everything. Think of the airless silence before the armored grasshopper
splits open & another grasshopper, ruthless, twice as big,

steps out.
              Some animals grow at a steady rate, & some by fits & starts.
When I am pure of heart, maybe I write for a thoroughbred in the last furlong,

and for a sparrow huddled in the freezing rain....
                                    When I try
to become deaf to what rustled between us—
                                    the thing that wind always kept

trying to tell us that it was—
                        I imagine how I'll be: a dark, numinous flatness
like an unpressed disc, re-markable, but less,
                                a creature half my size.

Three

On Jan. 5, 2005, NASA noted a milestone:
10,000 days since Voyager 2's launch.

This morning Neptune arrives through my computer:
                                                            the most beautiful image
 in the Solar System, you write, romanticizing, just a bit,

your attachment. The drama of the deeply non-human is so slow
it escapes me. Taken by Voyager 2 in 1989, the planet captured today

would look the same: a swirling giant—
                                        blue methane gas, clouds
& its own persistent storm, The Great Dark Spot, shaped like the red bruise

in Jupiter's sky. The descendant of the augurer & haruspex
is how Benjamin described the photographer. *The scene of a crime,*

he said, of Atget's eight thousand heavy 7 x 9-inch glass plates.
But doesn't any snapshot stop a thing dead?
                                        I'm traveling.

The hotel is almost empty: Saturday, just off a highway of corporate parks.
In the lot, an abandoned gray van, its windshield smashed, rests oddly

across the tidy lines. Can we imagine
                                missing this? Wanting a photograph
to document that cluster of garden apartments behind two rows of stunted pines?

What's more embarrassing than loving

       the obvious? What if you'd sent me
Venus or Saturn's rings? Atget, too, wants for obscurity. But I can't stop looking

at the reflections in the door-glass & shop windows: bare branches & white sky
above the slender samovar, a shelf of bottles & the flowerpots
           inside,

& Atget himself, the thin legs of his awkward tripod & the anachronism
of the camera's drape—even then—inserting itself between and over

the two blurred faces—they've been moving!—
        looking out. Later, you write:
To understand blues, you must understand breathing. And I suddenly see you,

slightly drunk, unearthing the old vinyl, turning up the volume, pleased, for now,
to be completely alone. When you insist that Duane Allman's improvised solo—

In Memory of Elizabeth Reed, Live at the Fillmore East—depends on
varying the *room* between notes,
      I think you must be talking about *timing.*

Is the edge of the galaxy any more remote than this street in 1908: dark cafes,
a drum, an iron deer, a baby Bacchus, hung up above the signs? Given a century,

wouldn't we reach it? Atget's head has been lost in the glass's confusion—
mirror & membrane—swallowed up in the round gaze of the woman—

is it a woman?— on the right.
     Voyager, its pockets full of old *hellos,* is slipping off
into interstellar-space.
     In the end, it's still a matter of distance, how far

we will go to bring something back. Neptune & its eight cold moons
are four & a half thousand million kilometers from the Sun.

Beneath its atmosphere, it has—like the second, spilt open & emptied—
no core.
        We cannot foretell the future but go on, instead, like Benjamin's angel,

predicting the past.
                Once I thought each day would be another day
for misfortune.
                The photographer would fail again to erase himself,

to become only an *eye*. But, surely, Atget means for us to find him, means
for us to go on finding him, again & again,
                                preserved in preserving

an almost-vanished world. *I can claim to possess all of Vieux Paris,*
he wrote, offering his archive to the State.
                                ...beautiful facades, beautiful

woodwork, the door knockers, the old fountains....
                                To inscribe ourselves
in what we love—into ragmen & wheels, the watch & the measuring stick—

& to be inscribed
                in turn. Is there a more perfect metaphor for this?
The black swath of his workcoat falls like a winter scarf below her chin.

Mysterium Cosmographicum

> *The roads by which men arrive at their insights*
> *into celestial matters seem to me almost as worthy*
> *of wonder as those matters in themselves.*
> —Johannes Kepler

Because I've forgotten the holiday, I arrive at noon to find a line of visitors—
so many children off from school—extending already through the lobby,
spilling past the revolving door.

>> They're queued to look at dinosaurs,

or butterflies, the meteorite, those moon rocks,

>>> or, perhaps, *The Birth of Time*

in the planetarium. Does it matter if I've never seen a hummingbird?
The ones inside have been dead for years, stilled to the stitched, iridescent

shimmer of Montezuma's feathered cloak or the 400,000 jeweled carcasses
auctioned off one week in London

>> to become handbags and hats. Yet—

who wouldn't be struck by this?

>> Our merciless wonder at the ordered

anatomies, the given & the made.

>> Each winter, ruby-throated hummingbirds

migrate—

> beyond our ken, without food or rest—500 miles across the Gulf,

but I was raised by a woman

>> who was afraid to leave her home.

Tucked in my aunt's tiny kitchen, I rarely got farther than off for a nap
or out,
            onto the porch, to turn the rusted wheel of the clothesline's pulley,
pinning shirttails & sleeves with black wooden pegs. In 1595, Kepler

designed a solar system governed by geometry, folding the flight of the planets
into a puzzle of perfect solids & spheres. The mind of God
                                                        did not speak to him
in words, but numbers.
                        Most hummingbirds live in the tropics, & some

weigh no more than a dime. I read this first in a picture book I studied
at my child-sized desk beside the stove. The living rate of an animal
depends on its size.
                    The metabolism of hummingbirds is so quick

no one understood
                    how it didn't starve to death while it slept. Einstein offered,
Either nothing is a miracle or everything is.
                                    In his home in Pasadena,
Robert Moore assembles a collection: behind glass, the preserved specimens—

blossomcrowns & sapphires, rainbows, comets—& pearl-sized eggs
like pairs of earrings
                        drowsing in their velvet boats. Nests as small
as coat buttons lined with thistledown & milkweed, sycamore wool,

encased in lichens,
                    & still sewn to a twig with a spider's silk. Because
my uncle was a builder, I learned to sort the fasteners. Bright headless nails,
wood screws, the glazer's points—
                            each slipped its quiet chime

into a labeled jar. Kepler once pondered a celestial music—the ratio
between the speed of Jupiter & the speed of Mars, a minor third;
the ratio between Earth &Venus, a minor sixth,

but the hummingbird

has no song. Its call is the flash & whistle of its wings. It hovers
among flowers & feeders

& it seems right. Today, there is a new force

at work in the galaxies, a cosmological constant that keeps the constellations

from collapsing into one another's arms.

A dark energy really does

pervade the vast emptiness of space: Einstein's earliest idea,
a balance for gravity's allure. Of course,

no narrative is the same

after a lapse of time,

or perhaps, we are no longer the same interpreters.

Yet, I recall those days as though they were filled with the story
of no story, the composition pitched to the leisure of dough rising

in a draped blue bowl. Does it matter

that we can never catch infinity? Or

that there might be an infinity within things for which we have

no sound?

That necklace of zeros. Measure after measure of the open string,

the white-mouthed whole note toward which the scales portend.

If we knew

what it was we were doing, Einstein wrote, it would not be called research.
Driven by an inspired delusion,

Kepler charted precisely the elliptical orbits,

constructed the equations that could solve their eccentric anomalies
for sense.
In the desert tonight, a scientist reads the heavens' radiant sigh, traces
the light-histories of exploding stars
halfway back to creation's start.

My aunt claimed I was a chatty child, but if we ever spoke, what did we have
to say?
Rather, I was stuffed in that silence with a lost, patient joy. Is it
by chance alone we ever find the pattern
we seek? Oliver Pearson discovered

the hummingbird hibernates each night. Only in this way can it slow itself
sufficiently to stay alive.
He watched as one of the Anna species settled down
at dusk on the branch of a tree. Returning at 3 am, he just reached up

& picked it. The moonlit answer
dreamt for hours in the cradle of his palm.

Physics

Because the rich fiber of marrow crosses at right angles
everywhere within us, the hollow femur & buried radius
are not as strong. All day I think about force
& what I remember of physics: the laws of inertia
& gravity, each unit the measure of one apple's weight.
Stress on the lintel, the concealed mystery of a loaded beam.
I know people who practice *feeling*. They try to prepare
for the loss of a father, a lover, how it might feel
when they themselves are gone. Chogyam Trungpa wept
when he learned the monk who had raised him
had been shot by the Chinese. This particular illusion,
he told a crowd, is very sad. I study a photograph
in the paper, a tent full of men—some in plaid shirts
& dark trousers, some in white robes—waiting
beyond the gates of a prison for word of brothers & sons
being held inside. The thin cotton roof appears
strung with petals, leafy acanthus & roses screened
onto curtains & sheets. Each news column gives us
the world in our own image: the cracked ribs of a dam
in Siberia, a fallen terminal in France, the derelict
Cowtown Inn in Fort Worth. Our impossible blueprint.
Each living bone carries more than it can bear.

Das Passagen-Werk

The first structures made of iron served transitory purposes:
covered markets, railroad stations, exhibitions.
                              —Walter Benjamin

On the top shelf of the closet, someone—
                              the last resident, or the one before—
has stored up cards of bobby pins, coat buttons, & the thin lathe
& bakery thread of old kites.
                    But the wind remains
unboxable.
          I'm trying to be through with things, to sign on

for the invisible. The various species of small desire, perhaps, we preserve
in the dim diorama of the chest. If we know they are there at all,
they're nothing—
               taxidermy of absence
announcing that this is where what we want would be,
                                        if only

everything were possible.
                    We are the ambitious arcade-makers
who cannot get it right: our media betray us. *Glass before its time*
& *premature iron*:
               an architecture of metaphor, of longing
& constraint.
          The sharp-boned corset was a cage, & emptied on the floor

beside the bed, it became a ruin, the collapsed rafters
of the waist.
          But isn't the body an arcade, too?

Not some close crawlspace or blind roof to cover what we are—
but a crystal palace,
                    the warm, tactile marketplace

for all that does not last. *The most brittle and strongest
materials.* Is it a question of morals
                              to want to touch all we can?
There are words that house in their meanings the notion of the temporal:
fairground & *carnival*. Diversion, the crooked street where no one

belongs. What issues is always *passage*:
                              whether we think we're moving
or not. It doesn't matter what avenue we choose.
                                        Four a.m.
on a dune in November, & I am here because
I said I would be. I set my clock to see the meteors extinguish themselves

on schedule in the atmosphere above the sea.
                                        I'd like to tell you
that in a year from now I'll still remember how I feel today,
but what was I thinking then on my back in the sand? There's so little
honesty in the world.
                    Not all the light that falls through the girded panes

is *dirty and sad*. It's that, but it's that
                              & something more.
To clean the eaves I need the desk lamp
& the extension cord. Far back against the chimney… what?
Another suitcase,
              some broken screens. In the dark, it's easy to believe

the earliest arcade must have seemed like heaven: transparent
interior, vaulted hall with a ceiling that disappeared. All obvious
pleasure—
          speck-swirl in shafts of sun, &…

after the stalls closed, a crinolined moon, its luminous hoop hung up
on a metal beam—
                          & promise. First, the rail station,
with its small altar of happiness at the intersection of the tracks,
& the hot house, & the exhibition…
the dusty fata morgana of the winter garden.

The Letters: A Mnemonic for Forgetting

T is for the Twofold

> The basic words are not single words but word pairs.
> One basic word is the word pair I-Thou.
> —Martin Buber

1

I walk out of a bookstore in Boulder & then go back. I don't want
to buy another book
              I'll never read: the correspondence of Nellie Sachs

& Paul Celan. I don't want to waste the money. I pass up an illustrated
Lives of the Saints, not wanting to carry the historic & tragic away with me

on a plane. I've already chosen a postcard, an elephant from Earl's Court Circus,
1928, holding a man by the head in its mouth, & a collection of photographs,

dead things,
              specimens forgotten in the backrooms of zoology museums.
But the jacket's bronzy detail lures me—
                      Rembrandt: Jacob Wrestling the Angel,

a story I suddenly fear
              I must be remembering wrong. *Du,* she must have chosen
to address him finally, writing from Stockholm to France:
                  Two handwritings

*are left to me in which the letters glow…. One belongs to my friend Gudrun,
who saved my mother's life and my own. The other*
                belongs to you. Without

the German, who can be sure? But I think *Du*.
                                              Thou. And I think
of the precision of those languages that make this closeness clear. Where I live,

                                    2

you can enter an elephant, climb the spiraling steps in its hind leg
into a perfectly plastered, peptic pink hull. There was another at Coney Island,

& a third, unfinished in Cape May, but now
                                              there is only this
building—its thousand tiny timbers, its epoxied tin skin—one eye

on the left, looking out, as it always has, across the ocean, & the right,
amblyopic & modern, locked on unadorned cinderblock apartments,

their serial aluminum railings, windows, doors.
                                              Some things are simply
too heavy, too big. If the skull of an elephant were not porous,

the animal would lack the strength to lift it from the ground.
                                              Dear,
wondrously deep poet Paul Celan, Sachs begins, *I inhale your work....*

It lies beside me on the table and when the night is too hard to bear, the lamp
is lit and I read again. Paul Celan, dear, dear, Paul Celan, you are coming

and then I will be in my homeland, whatever sand we may be standing on.
Imagine the un-lonely
                        loneliness of St. Joan. We tell ourselves she must have

wanted it that way. Though few, in their politics & faith, in their pleasures, want
to be so singular, so spare,
>   to have for comfort only the voices in their heads.

In a gallery, I watch an elephant on a video loop perform the trick of playing dead,
& each time,
>   its resurrected movements seem miraculous: the opening & shutting

of its trunk, its tender stare, a slow blink, each luxuriant twitch of the tail.
>   *If only*

I could give you something of beauty…
>   *but there is nothing to be found….*

I thought it was love;
>   it looks so much like an embrace. Yet we are assured
it is struggle & that at sunrise as Jacob left Penuel, he limped—sore

but certain he'd seen the face of god & been spared.
>   *Du. You at night busy*
unlearning the world…. But they could not unlearn it.
>   You & I, we don't know

the first thing about darkness, about terror, or the stake.
>   *We just don't know,*
you see, she tells him, *we just don't know what counts….*
>   Foolish indulgence.

What is it again I'm trying to forget? I could afford to convince myself
I needed you. I will afford to convince myself I don't.

Four

In a blue gallery, jarred like wax beans from a summer garden
& labeled *infiltrations*—the sounds that never belonged there:
the click-clack of the neighbor's high-heels in the hallway,
a garbage truck's whine. Harry Callas & Richie Ashburn
announcing the Phillies' starting line-up in the spring of 1972,
but also, birdsong & wind. The rustle of pigeons nested
between an air conditioner & a metal awning, their whirring purrs
& coos. In a glass case, the slick, rubber muscle of the bullfrog,
which leapt once out of a strange encompassing blackness
& tangled itself in the long hair you haven't had in years.
On the wall, the payphone you cannot dial correctly.
On a shelf beside it, the fumbling fingers of your rushing & the fist
of your getting it wrong. An inexhaustible pocket of dull, heavy coins.
Every room gives onto every other room. A wedding cake city
of Victorian hotels the size of skyscrapers, white clapboard
& gingerbread, all the porches deserted, the dark green shutters
closed. And, beyond, a cabinet for your confusion, excavated
from a municipal stairwell you climb or descend, now methodical,
now frantic, always looking for some way out. Chloroformed
& pinned to velvet, your effortless, acrobatic flying
& your gill-less, underwater breaths. Everywhere: the voices
you'd thought you'd forgotten. In the Great Hall,
like a Hollywood back lot, the doorways in which you have hidden,
terrified, from so many unseen pursuers & the doorways
in which you have unfolded, the frames against which
unlikely lovers have had you pressed. Here is the shadowy portal
from which you have just now awoken, your heart so loud
in the gray light of morning you are afraid it will give you away.

From Fragments

Many who have learned from Hesiod
the countless names of gods and monsters
never understand that night and day are one.
                    —Heraclitus

Sunday morning in the bath, I put the soap on the ledge, & it slips away.
I try again. It slides. It won't stay where it's always been.

It's a little slapstick—how long it takes me to find out
                                        what doesn't work.
Seeing his father for the first time, Telemachus mistook him

for a god. And growing in the boy for twenty years—undwarfed
by even one dry season of what a father really is—perhaps
                                        he had

become one. Telemachus had no memory
                        of this man, but he had seen gods—
gods pretending to be men.
                    Today, in the parking lot, a man slaps his son,

shoves him, until another man comes out to make him stop. Some fathers
are monsters, but mine was not one of these. When I studied Greek,

he wanted me to teach him the curses, some things he could say
Thursday nights at cards.
                    Things keep their secrets, I suggested.

What is scattered gathers. But he was
                                unimpressed. *The beginning*
is the end.
                Telos, the old noun, comes back from the dead. We tend

toward what we will become.
                                Maybe Telemachus should have
done something sooner: forced his mother to marry, forced her

to finish the shroud. He might have raised an army, challenged the suitors.
At least, he could have died trying. Do our fathers see us

when they've gone? I've forgotten
                                almost all the Greek I knew. Here
is the whole of my lexicon: this word for the inevitable & that other word,

logos, still on the tongue. Not a sign, a sign for sign. Not even the name
of a thing, only a word
                        for *word*. The feet at the end of the tub

are my father's feet, my feet through his, two diminished translations.
I thought one day I would know more & be changed by that. I thought

I would just step away into that other world, that place where living
happens.
        I do not forgive myself how little I know of the adventure,

the gamble, the bet.
                This is not princely. Odysseus speaks.
Here is the father his boyhood lacked. *No other Odysseus will ever come*.

Thinking of the Summer Solstice on the Longest Night of the Year

> The eternal return of all things has long since become
> childhood wisdom, and life an ancient intoxication
> of sovereignty, with the booming orchestrion
> as crown jewel at the center. Now the music
> is slowly winding down; space begins to stutter,
> and the trees start coming to their senses.
> —Walter Benjamin, "The Carousel"

/

The late train's arrival trips the streetlights on, a halogen morning timed
to last as long as it takes
                                to get from the platform to the lot.

But, walking home,
                        I can cover only half a block before the clock runs out
& it's night again. Here, the puddles are frozen, & ahead,

under the traffic signal's yellow flash—
                                                no hour to expect anyone
to stop—a blinking patch of broken ice. The electric lines buzz,

but it's a sound so persistent
                                it's silent—like a late June ebb, the marsh
at dusk so thick with crabs it thrums.
                                Benjamin loved the *abandoned,*

ramshackle summerhome in his childhood garden in Berlin,
its stained-glass windows—
                              passing from one colored pane

to the next, I was transformed. And the moon, he says,
unhoused him. Sometimes on a warm evening

I won't speak to anyone. I go alone into the reed-mace,
& no one sees. I become transparent. I strip down
                                          to underwear

& boots
          & disappear. Last night, the waitress at Maureen's,
a childhood friend, called out *Kathy K., Kathy K.*

repeatedly across the bar
                          because this is how she knows me, because
in grade school there were three other girls with the same first name.

In the crowd waiting for tables, a woman tells her date
she's happy for now
                    just taking the pills. *I don't want no one,*

she says,
          messing around inside my heart. He's worried
about his pick-up, the tools in the back. *You know*, he says,

sometimes you can just feel
                              when something strange might happen.
We can't stop believing this matters, or else we believe

it doesn't matter at all: a roadside motel, an amusement pier,
the Tilt-a-Whirl, the ferris wheel, the garishly buttoned saddles

of the two-tiered carousel—
                              the details, the things we've known
all our lives—
            wherever we've lived, above Budd's Floor & Tile perhaps....

And our afternoons, our tiny expeditions, the way our mothers sent us off
to the grocery for milk, or to the five & dime

for hem tape, Coats & Clark thread, tucking into one pocket
a dollar
        & into the other the scraps of cotton they wanted us to match.

And beyond ornament whatever endures—
                              the obliterating neutral:
landscape,
        the hard, muddy palette of a blasted wash. Oh—

maybe it wasn't like that for you, & I'm going on about a place
you've never seen, a place you wouldn't....
                              I mean, how could anyone

                              2

understand?
            Benjamin recalls the tinfoil wrappers on the chocolate,
brimstone butterflies with superbright wings, & the careful,

radiant sheen of bubbles.
                              My father re-did our bathroom with the samples,
no two ceramic squares exactly alike. But the border was black

& serious. Once he shook me awake in the dark
because he wanted me to see—
                              on our small, snowy television—men

bouncing across the surface of the moon. They're 238,857 miles
from the spot they left, & I'm afraid.
                              What does it mean, I ask him,

if they don't get back, they'll die?
                              Benjamin stands beside his mother
on winter afternoons as she sews, *surrendering now and then*

to the temptation to dote… on the underside, which with every stitch…
became more tangled.
                              Glitter. At the corner, what seemed like ice

is shattered glass. Who could tell by looking?
But when I kick a piece, I recognize the way it moves, the shallow clink

against the curb.
                              They've just re-poured the sidewalks
in aqua & turquoise swirls. It's a revision of a city,

but I don't believe it, the way we find ourselves suspecting
every renovation is a lie.
                              At twenty-one, I thought I could escape

myself—pedal off before dawn past the fish plant & kneel down
beneath the bridge. All summer the turtles came in on the tide,

clawed the bank, delivered up

                      the ripe, gelatinous clutch. The earth
lit by moonlight is *a counter-earth, an alternate*

to the one we know: unmapped bed of fluke & sucker, lost spoonbait,
catacomb of lure.
                Graber, so much like *graben*, the grave.

When I slide in beside him, my husband, in his sleep, puts his hand
over mine.
            We get used to the darkness. So much night in winter

its own illumination. *Why the world?*
                     Why this *abandon?*
What we feel is rarely balance, but an extravagance of shadow

& light, the spool
           of loud silk & its *hollow core*. I walk around
an unlocked gate, two open palms—
                how lonely the sufficient are—

when I press them to my ears… *like an empty shell, what do I hear?*
All the dead calling me
           my secret name, ridiculous & true.

The Letters: A Mnemonic for Forgetting

H is for the Hidden

> The elemental and intimate do not declare themselves
> openly. As a result, what is truly essential remains unsaid.
> —Lou Andreas-Salome

/

All night the restless August voices drift up from the street
                                        then drop away.
Under different circumstances, a man says. *Yes*, a woman pauses,

then repeats what he's said. Rilke, in an early letter to his beloved,
recalls the squirrels he raised as a child: *I bought long, long chains*

so that their freedom might come to an end only in the very high treetops.
It's taken me weeks to understand: what the poet wanted was to be bound

across great solitudes. In a new book, I read *nothing hurts so much*
as loving too much/ that which doesn't move among this world, but this I know

is wrong. She writes of Rilke: *We were not two halves seeking the other:*
we were a whole which confronted that inconceivable wholeness.... Yet

this cost her almost nothing to say, for she was, by then, confessing
merely to the void. I confess:
                    sometimes, still, this urging—

to lift your shirt just this bit to warm my hands, to place one red palm flat
against the tight heat of your chest & the other....
                            My niece dreams I speak

in numbers. Last night I said *Twelve. Twelve.* And she could tell I really meant
everything I said.
                    There it lies, Rilke describing Rodin's studio

at Meudon, its *indescribable blizzard of plaster casts: yard upon yard,*
only fragments, one beside the other… as if an unspeakable storm…

passed over this work.
                    It's not the intangible that torments us, but
what's right here: the familiar currant, abundant,
                                        beyond our grasp.

About *The Gates of Hell: one forgets they are only parts, and often parts*
of different bodies
                    that cling to each other so passionately there.

Rilke dedicated to Orpheus the memory of a white cart horse they had seen
together, *that clumsy-shackled gallop (how he greets you, Lou!),*

in the Russian twilight.
                    What was it about the cart horse, she asks, *returning*
to his nightly herd with a punishing wood block around one leg?
                                        For Xenocrates,

the soul is a self-moving number, but centuries later, who can re-construct
the fractured texts or decipher his intent?
                    At the city zoo, a little girl climbs the rail

3

& reaches.

   Sanguinus Midas. This morning she wants to bring the monkey
home— .

   in her ferocious wishing, her wrists of beads & bangles click together

the colors of macaws: green-headed,

        hyacinth-ed, yellow-winged. He can lie
in her bed at night, his bright hands clutching painted jewels, his dark tail

unsleeping

   around the waist of a doll. I submit the long thread & paper cup
of a childhood telephone. *Here, Lou—*

      Rilke names her again & again—

is another of my confessions.

     I whisper into the expanse with no hope
I will raise you.

   What has happened *un-happens*, & we re-write it. We assemble

that version we think we can bear. *Dear Lou, you were so truly the door
by which I first came into the open; now I keep coming… and place myself*

straight against the jamb.

    The only antidote for death remains desire,
even though it tears us. Once upon a time, I fell through a deep cold,

into this tended field,

    the immaculate furrow of your arrested gaze.
If my strumming is approximate…, well, I hardly know how to be more plain.

Five

Another Postcard

On this one: *Apples Grown by Irrigation at Artesia, NM.*
And under the caption, *Jimi A.* has scrawled *Miss Annie—
How are these for apples!* The year is 1907,
& Jimi's brown letters have the imprecise corona
of a leaky fountain pen. It's not much of a message,
is it? Although it says by its being *I'm thinking of you.*
Something this simple still brings you to mind. A yard
of apples, not a backyard, but 36 inches, a pyramid of them,
gleaming. And written out below each, the measured
fullness: 15 1/2, 16 1/2, 18, 20 oz. We're always tempted
to suspect the temptation. But this is a plot from Plato:
another party with too much wine. Resourcefulness
lies down with Want, & she conceives the god of desire—
though he will be plain & unshod & fated to sleep alone
at night in a ditch beside the road under an empty sky.
Just wise enough to be restless, chasing after the beauty
he does not have. Or, more likely, there's really nothing
much else Jimi wanted to say. Miss Annie being the spinster
who was always baking pies for the church sale, who lived
in the shingled house, with the climbing orange roses,
down the block, back home. And what's any of this got to do
with us? *Total weight, 12 lbs.* The answer's printed cleanly
on a placard to the right. Someone's taken the time,
done the math. It's a careful arrangement. Cultivation.
This balance of apples. Their variety unannounced, the photo
uncolored, they're so round they might be tomatoes, though,
here & there, a shadowy stem-dimple faces the camera
like a belly button, an open mouth, a scar. And the last one—
teetering atop all the others—holds forever its few dark leaves.

The Horse Latitudes

You think the winter sky—beyond the drafty window, half snow cloud,
half bleached light, not spilling on a tired delta, but, blown, instead,
against the eight dark floors of Keepers Move-and-Store—is on the brink

of telling you something important, but you wouldn't know how to read it,
even if it somehow learned to cast the right vowels. When an illustration
of the hook of Cape Cod, a black smear in a dictionary of geography,

looks, to you, like a detail from a Rorschach blot, you understand
you're working backwards: the shape of the specific dissolving
into the shape of nothing at all. Here, in your hometown,

the Atlantic spins between the pine slats of a storm fence.
The bedside clock gathers its net of nervous fish.
You try to remember the movies you watched in high school—

stretched out beside your father's chair on the floor of the den—
The Birdman of Alcatraz & *The African Queen*, & once Maggie Smith
as Miss Jean Brodie. It's not true that what you've feared most

has happened. This is merely the expected, though it doesn't feel
the way you thought it might. You can't call up the ending,
only that one scene of her lover, the artist, after she's spurned him,

painting yet another portrait of Jean. He must have come to wish
he'd never met her: the one region of regret you have all your life
foresworn. Years ago, you were in love with a man but couldn't tell him.

It wasn't the same for him. What would have been the point?
A Bernd & Hilla Becher photograph of a minehead in Sunderland
looks not like your brother's metal building set but its tinny music,

the frail jangle of unbolted arms being swept back, before dinner,
into a bright red box. A grain elevator in Elliot, Illinois
reminds you not of the pantry's stacked cans but of a shudder—

a torn sack being emptied from the bottom up. The sudden letting go
of burlap & seed, or the final shift into sleep, a pillow of shushing
buckwheat hulls. The pale cylinders of your own calves

against the morning's riptide, the familiar untucking of the sand
under your heels. Between the Trade Winds & the Westerlies
are the Horse Latitudes, sub-tropical belts of calm, dry air.

Here is where the ship's crew tosses the animals overboard—
when the passage has been unduly prolonged. You will go down
with the cargo. In the topography of fjords, you recognize a map

of veins. Southern Norway slips as low as your own heavy breast.

Pastoral

All winter I watched the cat in the butcher's window.
And now that the weather has turned & the door
to New Khan Meats stands open, I catch the whine
of the electric saw, the slap of the cleaver.
But because the white-coated workers stand
always with their backs to the street, I never have to see
what's being done. To keep ourselves together,
we learn to keep ourselves apart. Etched in the ancient tomb
of the Queen of Ur is the image of *Capra prisca*, a ram
caught in a thicket. We read the breed from the peculiar spiral
of its horns. The indifferent gray cat, loyal only
to the tough scraps from the master's block, slips out,
past two crates of mangoes, into the warm air of the stoop.
Last week, a man opened the battered back gate of an idling van
& swung three flayed goats—even the heads were bare—
across his shoulder, then stepped inside. The flesh
was neither pink nor bloodied, but a dry, articulate bank
of dark muscle & pale ribbons of fat. Imagine the first
spring, the fine, violet flank of night descending.

E is for Eros

> The beautiful is neither the veil nor the veiled object
> but rather the object in its veil.
> —Walter Benjamin

/

After the slaughter,
            sword drawn, Menelaus begins the search for his wife.
And who can blame him?
            Yet we still worship the heart—chambered geography,

ventricles, the few unsteady valves—
            at work in Helen, too. A young visitor
pursued her.
            She succumbed. And we shrug. Of course, there's more: a cuneiform

of causes, snow-melt feeding into the terrible rush of fate.
            How could she
have known so many would die as a result of her betrayal? Yet, when I can forget

what I know, I expect
            he will kill her when he finds her—no matter what
he feels.
            Where is she hiding anyway? In the furthest corner of Deiphobus's rooms.

Mythos: When the universe devoured half of all I loved, it burped up you. Mirror
& Consolation. Sometimes I forget the material,

the literal, fallible flesh we wear.

He sleeps in my arms,

Anais Nin writes of Henry Miller. *We are welded, his penis*
still in me.... I open my eyes, but I do not think. But I think. I think

we shall not touch: it is too late for me

to bare myself, & besides,
don't we already have everything we want? When Menelaus confronts her,

2

she turns, faces him calmly, lowers the neck of her tunic & exposes her breast.
Perhaps, just before,

she'd been remembering Paris. Perhaps she'd just slipped

another man's ring into the thick hem of her skirts.

I think she must mean
Here. This is where the blade must go. This is where the wound

already waits. I don't want to think she's simply performing some old trick:
that being Helen means

being spared. Perfect, from a swan's egg, she is

the impossible & the bottomless—but earthly.

No one gets another life.
I get letters from Henry every other day. I answer him immediately.

I gave him my typewriter, and I write by hand.

And without sacrifice,
how would we read the signs? The rising smoke, the entrails, the hurled stone.

It must have been from the pyre & the knife that we first learned to be severed
from ourselves & from
                    what would fill us, learned precisely how to paint
an expression of release.
                    Vermeer's *Head of a Young Girl* turns toward us
& turns away, her parted mouth too knowing; her eyes, seemingly

3

resigned.
          The truth is that this is the only way I can live—March 1932—
in two directions. I need two lives. I am two beings.
                              The price of inhabitation:

the blighted beauty of a limb—
                    on my desk, a pine branch with its bark stripped away,
& in the meat what is written are the engravers' marks—once, a voracious flood

of beetles,
          & now, this hieroglyphic river, the incised oxbows of a vacant bed.
I often return to this conflict—the passion for truth,
                              and also the passion for darkness.

I like best the Vermeer women who are lost to us
                              in what they hold. Private—
if they know we're looking, they don't let on: *Woman in Blue, Girl by an Open*

Window. There are other ways to be taken.
                              Or are these different lies I like to tell?
One: that we sometimes entered each other
                    in words. *I want to read Henry's letter.*

I excuse myself. I go to the washroom. I read the letter there. It is not very eloquent, and I am touched by that fact. Another: that I wouldn't have you,
                                                            even if....

More than matter, we are motion. Turbulent. Double—
                                    what wouldn't our bodies
unclearly say? Mutable desire. His fist opens; his weapon slips to the ground.

Beyond Saying

> *What finds its reflection in language, language cannot*
> *express. What expresses itself in language, we cannot*
> *express by means of language.*
> —Wittgenstein

A dozen children's drawings decorate a classroom window.
Kendra has filled her space with a purple rainbow;
Will, a flat road with a blue car. But Xiao, age 6,
has foreground: a larger-than-life brown bird on a squiggle
of grass. A small bright circle hangs in one corner
of the creamy construction paper sky, & a boxy house—
the size of a pat of butter—has been tucked into the distance
of a hill below the folded wing. I have no faith in my faith
that there are things beyond saying. The heart is so snug
in its careful home. I thought this might be a poem about America,
but here you come again, or the device of *you*, making it
personal, creating the perception there's some other reason
I might care. And, later, it will come down to a routine dawn
breaking into the hands of a magician's wife on an island
in the South Pacific. She's setting down palm frond boats of rice
along the edges of her garden: a daily offering to the spirits
who keep the shapeless wild apart from the tame. Last night,
in a small town in New Jersey, a wind-driven tide forced the ocean
up through the storm drains. And today, overlooked by the gulls,
a sunfish is disappearing. Stranded on the basketball court
of the community center, it is becoming, just past the foul line,
a platter of bones: translucent ribs still set into the round links
of its spine & the even-more-slender rays of a fin
fanning outward. Each fragile tine the width & anti-color
of the nylon tendons used to hold price tags to the crisp hems
of new sleeves. Things turn themselves into other things,

& words—it's true—are just the so-many unbodied, able assistants
of something else. We think the magician's wife must be thinking
of spells & the mysteries, but she is thinking instead of black ants,
which, occupied by these green vessels of grain, will leave
the household stores untouched. And she is thinking, too,
that she is herself capable of vanishing, of stepping to the left
of her own unfinished ritual, stepping into shadow,
just walking away. One spring, the same spring—why not?
Hasn't this become *our* story now?—that a woman on the edge
of a village kneels weighing the practical & possible,
a work crew digs a narrow bed in the cobblestones of the mews
so that another crew can come in & dig deeper. Then the plumbers
descend & do whatever it is that needs to be done. *We are the bees*
of the Invisible, Rilke writes to his Polish translator, meaning—
as if any of us can be sure—we must conjure from this world
our own cell of words. Two hundred heavy paving blocks
asleep for a week under a bright plastic tarp, & when I slip by,
I can feel them—meaning, merely, I know they are there.
If only a barking dog had distracted the workers, ...
this morning there'd be stone bookends on my mantle. Or—
and isn't this the point?—maybe I still thought, back then,
one for me & one for you. What doesn't grow to fit the tiny name
we give it? Here, take this: instead of a sweet chamber,
the sea's private letter, its stiffening envelope of hammers
& keys, an unremarkable fish, as delicately strung
as the rusting innards of an old piano, as thin & transparent
as a biology textbook's mylar page. Instead of a swarm
of bees rising fully formed from the liquefied bellies of bulls,
as they do in Virgil, there will only ever be these few,
overanxious, green-headed flies. Long ago I cut my brow
playing tag in the dark with a brother who is gone.
No one notices the scar. What scales remain are lifting.
Something large & abstract has been carried off in arms
too small to lift it. Sadly, this poem will have no consequence—

other than how we might render how it feels to summon
the old illusions we've somehow set aside. All the while
I've been afraid I might turn on you suddenly & say *sorrow*.
Or worse—say *love*. But, finally, even that ache is common
& un-tragic. A dumb, white slit of gill as remote & tender
as an opened curb. Something like perspective. Another shore.
Something like yellow light.

"Between Laurelton & Locust Manor" references a painting by Julian Schnabel.

The textual citations attributed to Benjamin in the poem "The Work of Art in the Age of Mechanical Reproduction" are taken from his essay of the same name. The poem also includes the names of Parisian Arcades. The quote by John Szarkowski comes from *Looking at Photographs*.

The italicized words in "Oracle" are from David Ferry's translation of Eugenio Montale's poem "La Farandola dei Fanciulli.".

Das Passagen-Werk is the German title of *The Arcades Project*, Benjamin's unfinished reflections on historical materialism and the phenomenon of the arcade in Paris in the Nineteenth Century. Most of the italicized words in the poem "Das Passagen-Werk" come from Section F of the *The Arcades Project*, [Iron Construction].

"From Fragments" includes bits of Brooks Haxton's translation of Heraclitus and Robert Fagles's translation of *The Odyssey*.

"Thinking of the Summer Solstice on the Longest Night of the Year," includes passages from Benjamin's essay "A Berlin Childhood around 1900" translated by Suhrkamp Verlag.

"The Letters: A Mnemonic for Forgetting": Each of these poems contains material from either a private correspondence or a journal or both. The quoted passages in "L is for Laburnum" are from Kafka's conversation slips. "E is for Elegies" is a tribute to Larry Levis and takes part of its title from his poem "There are Two Worlds." The epigraph is from an interview Levis gave between 1989-90," which appears in *The Writer's Chronicle* (Oct/Nov 2003). The italicized text is from Levis's letters to Phil Levine, and these are archived in The New York Public Library. The epigraph for "T is for the Twofold" is from Martin Buber's *I and Thou*. The poem has incorporated excerpts from the correspondence of Nellie Sachs and Paul Celan as well as fragments from the poems they dedicated to one another. "H is for the Hidden" contains excerpts from the journals and memoirs of Lou Andreas-Salome and passages from the correspondence between Andreas-Salome and Rainer Maria Rilke. The line "nothing hurts so much…" is from Christopher Cessac's poem "Fragments of a Letter to Christopher Smart." "E is for Eros" was inspired by an early draft of a poem by Matt Donovan, "A Blues about Wanting in the End," and its epigraph is from Walter Benjamin's essay "Goethe's Elective Affinities." The poem also contains passages for Anais Nin's *Diary* (1931-32).

Also Available from saturnalia books:

Winners of the Saturnalia Books Poetry Prize:
Lullaby (with Exit Sign) by Hadara Bar-Nadav
My Scarlet Ways by Tanya Larkin
The Little Office of the Immaculate Conception by Martha Silano
Personification by Margaret Ronda
To the Bone by Sebastian Agudelo
Famous Last Words by Catherine Pierce
Dummy Fire by Sarah Vap
Correspondence by Kathleen Graber
The Babies by Sabrina Orah Mark

No Object by Natalie Shapero

Nowhere Fast by William Kulik

Arco Iris by Sarah Vap

The Girls of Peculiar by Catherine Pierce

Xing by Debora Kuan

Other Romes by Derek Mong

Faulkner's Rosary by Sarah Vap

Gurlesque: the new grrly, grotesque, burlesque poetics
edited by Lara Glenum and Arielle Greenberg

Tsim Tsum by Sabrina Orah Mark

Hush Sessions by Kristi Maxwell

Days of Unwilling by Cal Bedient

Letters to Poets: Conversations about Poetics, Politics, and Community
edited by Jennifer Firestone and Dana Teen Lomax

Artist/Poet Collaboration Series:

Velleity's Shade by Star Black / Artwork by Bill Knott
Polytheogamy by Timothy Liu / Artwork by Greg Drasler
Midnights by Jane Miller / Artwork by Beverly Pepper
Stigmata Errata Etcetera by Bill Knott / Artwork by Star Black
Ing Grish by John Yau / Artwork by Thomas Nozkowski
Blackboards by Tomaz Salamun / Artwork by Metka Krasovec

www.saturnaliabooks.com